ACKNOWLEDGEMENT

I would like to acknowledge my dear friends, Robert and Julia, who started the journey of exploring cuddle positions and thought of making it into a book – but they had never gotten around to completing it. The image on the right was the only drawing that they created. Thank you for allowing me to take your idea and run with it. If it wasn't for them and my loved ones, this book would not have been written.

Thank you to everyone who helped me in the process of creating *The Cuddling Sutra* and supporting me. Especially my mother who has spent hours editing my grammar and Micky, who is pun-believably hilarious. For that - I give you some ***cuddles***.

TABLE OF CONTENTS

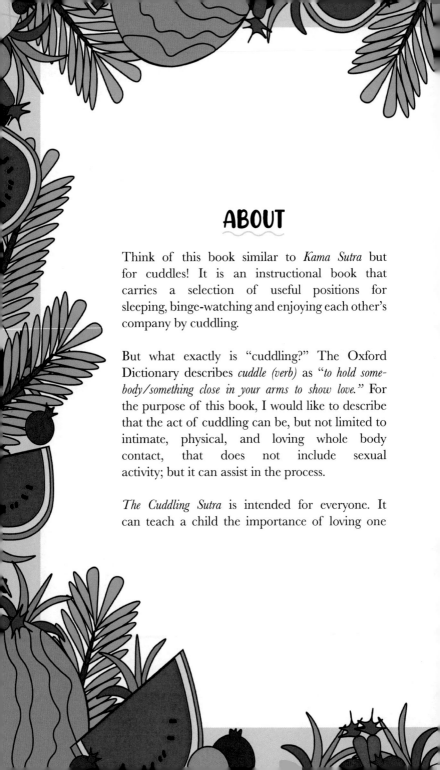

ABOUT

Think of this book similar to *Kama Sutra* but for cuddles! It is an instructional book that carries a selection of useful positions for sleeping, binge-watching and enjoying each other's company by cuddling.

But what exactly is "cuddling?" The Oxford Dictionary describes *cuddle (verb)* as *"to hold somebody/something close in your arms to show love."* For the purpose of this book, I would like to describe that the act of cuddling can be, but not limited to intimate, physical, and loving whole body contact, that does not include sexual activity; but it can assist in the process.

The Cuddling Sutra is intended for everyone. It can teach a child the importance of loving one another, building stronger relationships or diving deeper into intimacy.

"I just saw this new cuddling technique, can we try it out?" is a lovely way to ask your cuddling partner if they would like to cuddle. There are more positions to discover beyond this book. Even if you mess up a position, try different versions that suit your needs. Ensure that your friends are consenting and comfortable with a cuddle. What matters most is having fun.

Try these at your own risk - know your limits and listen to your body. *The Cuddling Sutra* is not responsible for any injuries or broken objects that may occur when trying these positions.

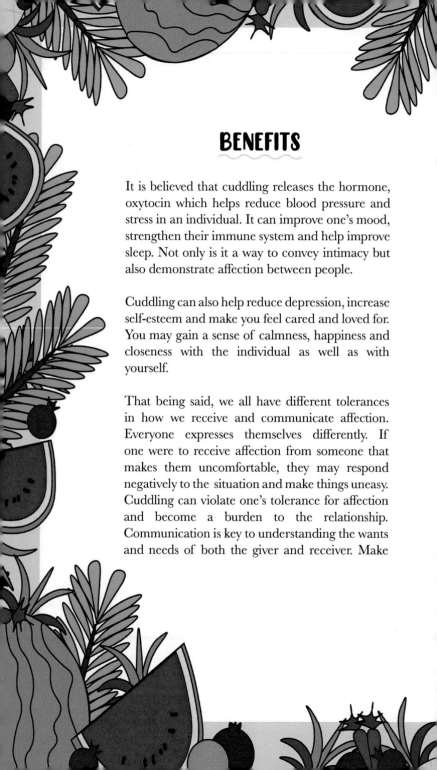

BENEFITS

It is believed that cuddling releases the hormone, oxytocin which helps reduce blood pressure and stress in an individual. It can improve one's mood, strengthen their immune system and help improve sleep. Not only is it a way to convey intimacy but also demonstrate affection between people.

Cuddling can also help reduce depression, increase self-esteem and make you feel cared and loved for. You may gain a sense of calmness, happiness and closeness with the individual as well as with yourself.

That being said, we all have different tolerances in how we receive and communicate affection. Everyone expresses themselves differently. If one were to receive affection from someone that makes them uncomfortable, they may respond negatively to the situation and make things uneasy. Cuddling can violate one's tolerance for affection and become a burden to the relationship. Communication is key to understanding the wants and needs of both the giver and receiver. Make sure that both are comfortable with the situation. You should cuddle at your own risk and comfort level.

There are endless opportunities to explore. Some positions are very common - some might not be. Cuddling is fun for all shapes and sizes. It is suggested that you experiment with your companion and not give up finding the PERFECT position. The human body is always changing. We grow in height and size, we shrink, our relationships change, and we have injuries over time. This might affect the degree of what feels comfortable and with whom we share these more intimate moments.

All these positions were created and intended for two (or more) people to enjoy, regardless of religious background, income, employment status, ethnicity, age, or sexual orientation. Keep in mind that some positions might be considered public displays of affection and frowned upon in some countries.

GUIDE TO

WHAT IS HUGGING?

Hugging is the most similar, common type of cuddling. It is a brief embrace between two individuals. However, the difference is that when you hug, it tends to be for a quick amount of time. It can range from 5 seconds to 5 minutes for example.

Many believe that short hugs have been associated with decreased levels of cortisol in the blood. With more frequent hugging, one might start to see a lower heart rate and blood pressure.

You can intensify the hug by adding more pressure and time.

ADD YOUR NOTES

_____

_____

_____

_____

_____

_____

_____

_____

GREETING HUG

Has a stranger ever hugged you before? Perhaps a stranger hugged you for the first time. Maybe you are hugging a friend quickly, as they enter your home before they take off their shoes.

A *Greeting Hug* can have many names: polite, quickie, hello, friendly, awkward… it is one of the most common hugs one would share with a friend, stranger, or colleague. This type of hug is not considered to be intimate and lasts for just a few seconds. However, one can extend the time, if desired.

HOW TO:
Extend both arms higher (or lower) than your hugging partner. One typically reaches for shoulders or goes under the arms, placing their hands on their mid-back. Be careful though! Extending your hands lower on the back, closer to the other person's behind may make them uncomfortable, or turn this hug into a more intimate one. One can hug with the choice of one or two arms!

If needed, you can extend the hug to show more affection and love by the intensity and duration. One can even rest their head on the shoulder or chest for more comfort.

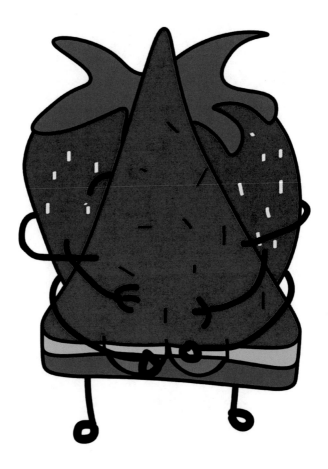

KOALA-TY HUG

Have you ever missed someone so much that you want to attack them with love? When it feels like it has been forever since you last saw one another? Or perhaps your partner and yourself are very passionate. The *Koala-ty Hug* requires a little more physical exercise and balance. Make sure that the person receiving the hug has a strong foot placement or else when you jump, you both will collapse and fall.

HOW TO:
Have the jumper wrap their hands around the other's neck and put all their weight onto the catcher as they jump up and wrap their legs tightly around. The most comfortable spot would be to have the jumper's legs above the hips. Have the catcher wrap their arms around the other's torso. If done correctly, the catcher can let go of their arms and still hold onto the jumper. However, if the jumper begins to run in your direction, make sure your hands are free, or place the objects down on the floor and brace for impact!

If it feels like the person is falling or slipping down, simply wrap your arms around under their legs, do a little squat and jump up, lifting their legs back to a comfortable spot.

CRISS-CROSS

It's sometimes hard to gauge where someone will place their hands on your body. Will they reach for the neck or go under the arms? This style of hugging provides a clever solution when unsure. Regardless, you will have a guarantee 50 - 50 chance of succeeding.

HOW TO:
Similar to the *Greeting Hug* - the *Criss-Cross* hug is more about the hand placement on the other's torso. Extend one hand around the neck, and the other on the waist. If you are lucky, your hands will interlock on the other person's back.

It is a lovely "I missed you" hug when back in your loved one's arms again. One may also feel the need to rest your hand on the other's shoulder and close your eyes. It will make the hug more intimate.

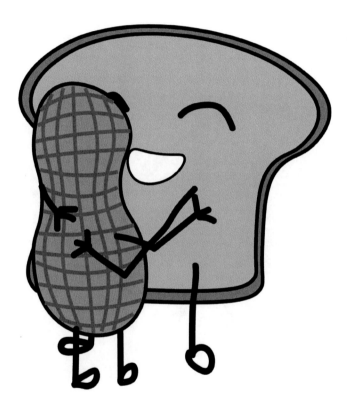

EYE WANT TO HOLD YOU

When feeling in a silly mood, and want to playfully make your loved one uncomfortable or engage in an eye staring competition - then this is the perfect position for you! The longer you maintain eye contact with your partner, the more they may start to question your behaviour or make them feel uneasy. Or maybe it is prom night and you want to slowly dance around in a circle, with your date! The position is intended for those who are more comfortable with one another. Do not greet a stranger with a long intense eye stare - it might freak them out.

A commonplace where one would see the *Eye Want to Hold You* is when two people are dancing with each other, or just want to have a "stare-off."

HOW TO:
When going for an embrace, simply stare face to face with one another, wrap your hands around the neck/waist of the person, and have a stare-off. The eyes are the gateway into the soul. Although this doesn't seem like an intimate hug, the practice of maintaining eye contact creates a deeper connection.

HEAD NOOGIE

There are many ways that lead into giving a *Head Noogie*. For example, while you are playing with your sibling and then all of a sudden, they take your favourite toy! Perhaps you're in a playful mood and want to engage in a tickle war with your partner. Maybe you want to show dominance or displeasure. This is meant to be a playful form of affection. The goal is NOT to create long lasting bruises. Please use caution with the *Head Noogie*.

HOW TO:
Approach your target from either side, wrapping your arm with your forearm and bicep, put your target in a headlock, tilting their head towards you (without choking them). With your free arm, create a fist and start rubbing your knuckles fast, across their head.

This is not to be used on a fresh perm or new hairstyle - it can anger the other and make them upset. The hair will not survive the hug, so make sure they don't get mad at you.

BACK WARMER

Is it close to a holiday? Birthday? Anniversary? Feel as if your loved one is hiding something? The *Back Warmer* is fun if you want to surprise your partner or if they have been acting weird. This can be used when your target is working on the computer, cooking, or some other form of activity. It can also be used as a sneak attack if one wants to spy on the other person without any forewarning.

HOW TO:
Approach your target from behind and wrap your arms over their shoulders. Squeeze gently and place your head on their shoulder for rest. The partner receiving the hug may wrap their hands over yours if they feel it is necessary.

KISS ON THE CHEEK

We've all been there - our first time when someone pulls you in close to their face. One must be thinking, why is this stranger so close? Why are they kissing me? What should I do with my lips? Do I kiss them back? Why does it sound like they are kissing me but are not? Fear not - we have the basics covered so you are prepared for the *Kiss on the Cheek*.

It is hard to tell when the person will go for a handshake, hug or kiss on the cheek. If you are travelling to a place with a different culture, make sure that you are aware of the different greetings they might have and be prepared.

HOW TO:
Once committed, gently place your hand on their upper arm, turn your cheek towards the other person and lean in. The question is lean to the right or left? That depends on the culture, although most will lead with their right cheek. You can kiss the person multiple times - although the safest will be one quick kiss. **DO NOT KISS THE PERSON ON THE CHEEK.** Rest your cheek against theirs and kiss the air.

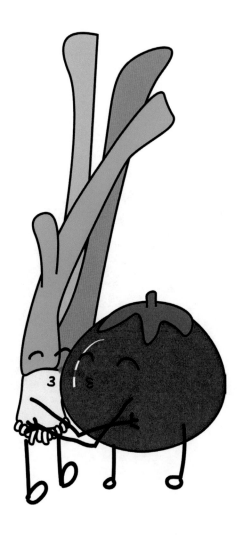

LONDON BRIDGE

Imagine that it is a nice summer day. Your friends and family are having a BBQ in the backyard. You notice that your neighbour is also enjoying the sunshine. You approach the fence to say hi and greet them - but the fence gets in the way! This hug is brilliant if there is a table, fence, or anything that prevents you from a full-body hug. It is also an outstanding form of hugging that demonstrates to the other person that you might not be romantically interested, as most of your body is not in contact.

HOW TO:
It is a type of hug where you use your upper body while keeping the lower part of yourself far apart from the other. This should create a lot of space between each other. Have one person wrap their arms around your neck and the other under the arms! You can also explore positions and try the *Criss Cross* here as well.

The *London Bridge* can also turn into a fun game with multiple people. Have them run between the space of the two huggers. The huggers will try and trap you with their love by using their arms. One might expect their arms to fall onto you - similar to the game of London Bridge.

THE COOKED SPAGHETTI

You're in another playful mood but need to change it up from the other positions? Do you feel you are having trust issues with your loved ones and want to test it? Have you ever hugged a child and they completely relax every muscle in their body to show that they want to be held and carried? Maybe someone skipped arm day at the gym? This position is a great arm workout!

The Cooked Spaghetti occurs when one person is hugging the other person and they go completely limp, relaxing all muscles. This can occur when the hugger is squeezing as tightly as possible, causing the other to go limp like a rag doll.

HOW TO:
Once you feel as if your loved one has a good grip and you are held tightly, simply trust that they will hold on as you completely fall into their arms, relaxing your legs and arms. Be careful if your loved one has a bad back - this might cause further pain for them. Make sure that they have a solid foundation first or you both might fall onto the floor and cause an injury.

It can be a fun trust-building exercise with your loved one. Will they let you fall to the ground? Or hold you tightly in their arms?

ONE SIDED

You've just left the store and your hands are full with groceries. A friend has spotted you in the parking lot and would like to hug but you don't want to drop your bags. All of a sudden, your friend takes their arm and holds you at their side. Wow, you think, this is amazing. "I didn't have to free my hands yet I can still enjoy their company and lean into their hug."

HOW TO:
One Sided occurs when both of you are facing each other or in the same direction. The person receiving the hug does nothing. Just let your arms hang by your side or continue with what you were doing while the hugger will take their closest arm, wrap it behind your torso, and squeeze tightly.

It is a safe, and friendly embrace - especially for those who aren't fans of hugging. It can also be a good form of communication on a job well done or a pat on the back.

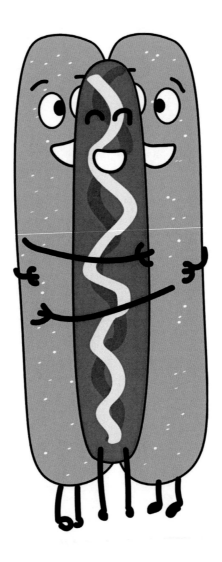

GROUP HUG

It's been a fun day outside, hanging out with your friends and creating beautiful memories. But now it's time to say goodbye. But there is a dilemma - there is more than one person to hug! You are in a rush and need to say a quick goodbye but still want to show you love them. Hug them all at once with this position!

HOW TO:
Simply sandwich the person between you and your friend, trapping them in the middle while everyone tries to hug around the inside person. *The Group Hug* can work with multiple people, just wrap your arms around the people beside you. The key to success is to have at least one person in the middle, while the people on the outside are making a *One Sided Hug.*

This can be a playful hug, trapping your friend in a love bubble. The middle person may have difficulty escaping. Ensure that everyone checks occasionally for breathing - we don't want to suffocate our friends.

SELF HUG

When you feel lonely, or just want to hug someone - why not hug yourself? Give yourself a pat on the back. We deserve some self love! A *Self Hug* is one of the many ways to demonstrate love and affection for yourself.

HOW TO:
All one has to do is wrap your arms around your torso, reaching for your back and squeeze tightly!

A fun trick to play on your friends is having your back facing them - give yourself a *Self Hug* and slowly move your hands on your back. This will create an illusion that someone else is embracing you or perhaps kissing you.

THE WHIRLWIND

You've been waiting at the train station for your loved one to arrive. It's an hour late and you haven't seen them in a couple of months. As the train pulls up, you are patiently looking for them. It's towards the end, the flow of people has slowed down. It feels like you've been at the wrong terminal. But alas! They are the last ones to leave the train. All your emotions take over and you charge at them, running at full speed into their arms.

HOW TO:
This type of hug needs a lot of speed and momentum. Have the jumper run towards the other and jump into their arms. The catcher should hold that person, using the momentum to spin them around. The jumper should place their hands around the other's neck. The catcher will place their arms under the jumper, wrapping around their torso. The jumper can lift their legs free, or kick them up towards their back while spinning. If your hands aren't free while they are running towards you, quickly place the objects on the ground and brace for landing. Make sure that the person holding you is standing firmly or else they might fall.

Be careful of objects around - you might hit them like a tornado.

THE NUZZLER

It's dark and stormy outside and you've been invited to a romantic dinner with your loved one. You've been longing for a warm embrace from your partner. It was a long, tiring day at work and all you want to do is snuggle up and be warm.

HOW TO:
Have one person wrap their hands around your neck while the other goes under their arms, onto their lower back. Here is where you can perform the neck hug. Take your head and nuzzle it into the other person's shoulders, and turn your head towards the other person. This will perform a hug for the body and head!

It is a safe form of hug but be careful, as your faces will be very close to one another. Make sure that you establish that it is a hug and nothing more, because if it is miscommunicated - it can become awkward if someone tries to kiss and you were not expecting it.

couch

WHAT ARE COUCH SNUGGLES?

Want to embrace the person sitting next to you on the couch while you're watching a movie, but don't know what to do? This section will give you some tips and pointers on making that move so that you and your partner are both comfortable with each other's embrace.

Make some popcorn and grab a blanket. These snuggles are not for the lighthearted!

ADD YOUR NOTES

_____

_____

_____

_____

_____

_____

_____

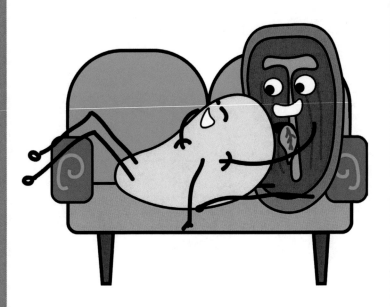

SOFA SPOON

You just got home from work or school and need to rest your feet. Your loved is one sitting on the couch, watching their favourite show or reading a book. You politely ask them to lay sideways, placing their feet onto the couch, and guide them to make room for you. After some time relaxing, you start to fall asleep, slowly drifting into your loved one's arms.

HOW TO:
This will only work if the sofa is long enough to fit two people or more. Start by leaning back into the sofa, with your feet up, spreading your legs apart, creating space for the other person. The other person will then fit into the space and rest their head on your thigh, stomach, or, lean back resting their feet up on the sofa as well. The person laying down can be on their back or side. Be careful though, you might make their legs turn numb.

Use caution when moving around, elbows are sharp and you might bruise one another.

SEAT SNUGGLE

You just witnessed your child or friend make a fool out of themselves and can't help but laugh uncontrollably with one another. As you laugh, you slowly fold into a fetal position towards each other, laughing and snuggling together.

HOW TO:

This is an expert position. You are combining a *One Sided* hug as well as using all four limbs. Have both people lean into each other, wrapping their arms around each other's back, facing the same way. One can have their feet on the couch or resting on the floor.

It is a perfect embrace for families until one starts to lose feeling in their body or become uncomfortable. This position is good when you still want to have the ability to use your hands.

COLD FEET

It's the coldest night of the winter. You've always wondered why you live in a cold part of the world. You've been longing for the warmth from the sun on your skin. You just came back from a hike and your feet are soaking wet. Your feet are freezing and you need to warm them up fast.

HOW TO:
Sit on opposite ends of the couch. Ensure that you can reach one another with your feet. Simply sit on the other person's feet to keep them warm, or play footsies. *Cold Feet* is a fun, playful way to enjoy each other while still having your space. Feet can become numb after some time; don't be offended if they pull their feet away prematurely. Bear in mind if your feet are freezing, it might upset your partner and might cause them to retreat to their side of the couch. Ensure your socks are clean and the other is comfortable with feet - this position is a touchy one so hold on!

LEG CUSHION

Just finished moving but still haven't unpacked all the boxes? You've spent three hours looking for where you packed your living room pillows. Perhaps you are living a minimalist lifestyle and are in need to rest your head without couch pillows!

HOW TO:

Similar to the *Sofa Spoon*, however, the person's legs are resting on the floor instead of up on the couch. Have the person lay down on the couch and rest their head on your thigh. If you want to show extra love - give them a little head massage too. Side of caution - they might fall asleep and leave your legs numb.

The person resting on your lap will have a glorious view of your cute little chin. So look into one another's eyes and smile!

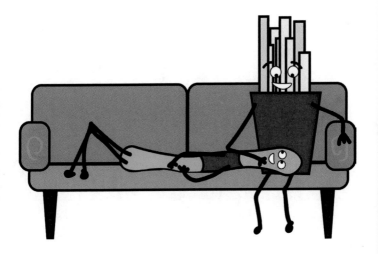

GETTING HANDSY

Imagine you are sitting in a movie theatre, one reaches for the popcorn the same time you do... and your hands touch. It is the first date; you are trying to figure out if the other person is into you. If they hold your hand after the popcorn, then it is a sign of success! If they retreat, perhaps it is time to leave that date behind!

HOW TO:

This position is good for hand holding - or if your partner keeps tickling you, simply grab and hold their hand. This can reduce the odds of being tickled, while letting them know you still care. If feeling extra loving, this position would be incredible for a slow hand massage. Only engage in the hand massage if you are comfortable with one another. If done on the first date, it might make the other person uncomfortable and scare them away. You need to be careful though! If your loved one is a clean person, they might be put off by oily, dirty hands when eating food.

WHAT IS BED SNUGGLES?

A bedroom can be a very intimate place. It's nice to balance romanticism with equal time spent cuddling and demonstrate affection. This guide to bed snuggling can be used in any situation where you find yourself with a partner in a bedroom, whether it's upon waking in the morning, before going to bed, or just for some afternoon delight.

Ensure you have an alarm set if your goal is not to fall asleep. These cuddles will send you into a trance and easily take you to dreamland.

ADD YOUR NOTES

_____

_____

_____

_____

_____

_____

_____

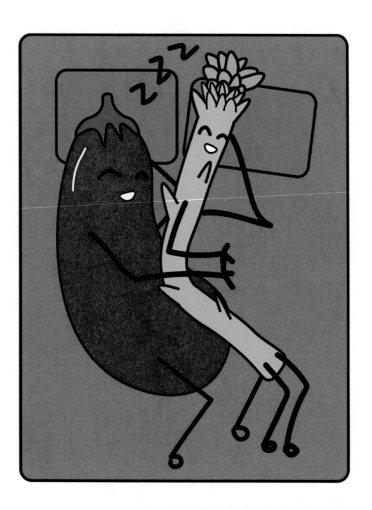

SPOONING

Spooning - we all have heard it but the question is do you know HOW to spoon? Are you choosing to be the little spoon or big spoon? This position is fantastic for slowly falling asleep in each other's arms, you can create different modifications to suit your needs.

HOW TO:
The little spoon will be facing away from the other, having their back towards them. The big spoon will be facing the other person's back of the head, wrapping their arms around them. Ensure that the little spoon is slightly higher than you. By doing so it avoids having hair in the big spoon's face.

The big spoon will lie on their side while the little spoon puts their back to the big spoon's stomach. It is important that the big spoon's top arm should wrap around the little spoon - the bottom of the big spoon's arm will fit wherever it is comfortable. The little spoon can lie on their side, or curl into a fetal position, bringing their feet up. If wanting to 'escape' this position - simply turn your back towards the little spoon.

CHEST REST

This is good for people who are enjoying each other's company and are not ready to fall asleep. If you do not have an office space, the position will be a perfect way to feel productive as well as let the other know you love them. If you aren't ready to sleep yet, one can talk, read or watch something together and still be working. This will only work if you have a large bed such as a queen or king.

HOW TO:
Have one person lay on their back comfortably, while the other lay horizontally and uses the other person's torso as a headrest. Do not push down with the head; it will be hard for the other person to breathe. If you have your hair tied up, keep in mind that it might create a sharp pressure point on their chest.

If it is uncomfortable for either party, place a pillow between the head and chest to promote a higher degree of comfort.

BUTT TO BUTT

You show up to the hotel room and there is only one mattress. You both awkwardly look at each other, trying to figure out the alternatives. Perhaps you are stuck sharing the same bed with a housemate or sibling. Your only option is to sleep in the opposite direction.

HOW TO:
Have your backs facing each other, sleeping butt to butt. This position is also good for when you want your own space, or, if the room is too hot, but still want to let the other person know that you care.

Some other variations - sleeping in the same direction and have your butts touch each other. One can also place a pillow between each other for extra space - just in case. It will create a platonic space when the only option is sharing the same bed.

CAN'T LET GO

Imagine spending the whole day with your loved one and you had a beautiful, romantic anniversary. You haven't seen them in two weeks and simply can't stop showing them love and affection. You keep staring at them or touching them to the point where you feel like squeezing them to death, similar to when you see a cute puppy. (Do not actually squeeze them to death - that is a big no-no.)

HOW TO:
Similar to the *Spooning* position but the 'big spoon' has their arm and leg entangled with the other person. They are simply almost restricting their partner's movement. Have the big spoon take one or both of their legs, bent at their knees, and go over one or both legs of the little spoon.

This is for those who just love too much and cannot contain their affection. Be forewarned, if the other person is trying to sleep, you might wake them up and create an unpleasant environment.

BODY SLAM

You've been having this feeling burn inside for a while - that type of feeling that makes your whole body itch and tingle. You cannot wait to 'go to bed' with your partner, although they are slowly falling asleep. You are desperate to let them know that you aren't ready to sleep yet. What to do? You *Body Slam* into them to let them know what is up.

HOW TO:
The *Body Slam* position is more on the intimate side. Face each other and fully press both bodies together. It can also be a variation for *Spooning* as well. The key importance here is that you use your full body pressed against the other person. Take your arm that is resting away from the bed and reach it around the other's back. Have the other arm either rest under your head or your partner's. Watch out or your arm can turn numb. The goal of the *Body Slam* is to not have it last as long. It can become uncomfortable quickly and get very hot.

Be warned, it can lead to something more than cuddling so set your boundaries prior to this position or you may confuse your partner.

ENTANGLED

Stuck laying awake in bed because your partner keeps moving around? Try trapping them into a position to prevent them from further movement so that you can get a good night's rest.

HOW TO:
Entangled is where you and your partner face each other, having your legs intertwined, with your arms wrapped tightly around one another. *Entangled* tends to leave more space between each other's bodies because you usually need room for your legs to be bent together.

This is a good position to show affection before sleep, without the risk of falling asleep. It can be uncomfortable in the legs after an extended period of time.

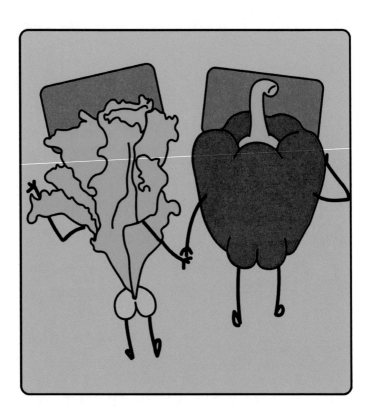

FACE DOWN

Need your own space? It is the dead of summer, with a high percentage of humidity in the air. If you or your partner are stomach sleepers or don't want to sacrifice your "cool bubble," then you may find that this position is a remarkable way to find comfort while battling the heat of the summer.

HOW TO:
Simply reach for their hand and hold it. It is a gentle reminder that you still want to let the other person know you care but you need your own space.

For something extra special, you can play with their fingers and give a hand massage to show that you really care about the other person. One can also rest your hand on their back, gently moving it up and down. This adds more comfort and lets them know that you are loving.

THE 96

Does your partner have bad breath and sleep with their mouth open? Are they snoring right in your ear? This is a refreshing alternative to show your loved one that you care for them - bad breath and everything. If the snoring prevents you from sleeping or you are breathing in their bad breath, this position is a temporary fix. However; if your partner is affecting your sleep, it would be beneficial to have a conversation about it.

HOW TO:

This position works when resting on opposite sides (feet where the head is). Both parties need to lie on their side, knees bent. Legs can either be stacked on top of each other or side-by-side, depending on how high the other wants their head to be rested. The other will place their hand on the other's body, similar to a headrest. You can place your hands where they feel comfortable. It only works if both people are facing each other. Keep in mind that your legs might be squished together or become numb after some time. Make sure that your legs are comfortable before the other rests their head.

THE NUMBER 4

Is your partner tired of cuddling you and wants their own space but you are not done with cuddling yet and still have a high affection level? This position is for those who enjoy cuddling but find it gets too hot for them and still want their space.

HOW TO:
The person next to you can be sleeping, they can have their hand resting under your neck or not. Simply take your closest leg to your partner, and bend your knee over one or both legs. Depending on your leg size and height, one would need to adjust your position to ensure that the leg that is hugging is comfortable. If your partner is feeling extra loving, they can place their hands on your thighs. This is an amazing position if you do not enjoy having your bodies touch each other while sleeping.

Keep in mind that some people will have a sensitive area between their legs. Do not apply pressure there and make sure that you are not making your partner uncomfortable or having their leg fall asleep.

CROSS BODY

You are the first person to wake up and start the day. However, you made plans with your loved one who is still sleeping and needs to be woken up. This position will slowly and gently wake them up. Just hold them and give them a gentle squeeze or move your hands up and down their side. Be careful - it might tickle them and cause an unpleasant wake up.

HOW TO:

Have the person rest their arm under your body. Take your farthest arm away from your partner, reach over and wrap it around their torso as well as your legs bending over theirs. One can be either lying on your back or side when doing this position. Once completed, rest your head on their chest if feeling extra cuddly. Be mindful that your hair might choke the other person, which will then make them uncomfortable.

ON TOP OF THE WORLD

Feel tired after giving your partner a massage? Perhaps you want to end off with a long-lasting cuddle, where you both slowly fall asleep. Maybe you are stuck sleeping on a smaller kid's bed or a twin bed and need room and space? What if you are camping in a cold place, where it is below freezing in the backcountry, and are in a one person tent?

HOW TO:

This position has multiple versions - face down, or laying on your back. The person on top can also face down or lay on their back. Doesn't matter what side. The key here is to find that sweet spot between both bodies. The chest is a good place to rest your head if laying chest to chest. Or the person's behind makes a good pillow, if resting on their back.

NEVER LET ME GO

Has your partner been asking for a back or neck massage for a while now? Did they have a night of poor sleep and they slept on their neck funny? This would be a delightful position to give them what they've been asking for. Surprise them when you are watching your favourite series together on your laptop or T.V.

HOW TO:
When the two of you are lying in bed and wanting to watch something, *Never Let Me Go* is for you! Have one sitting up, using the wall or bed rest to support their back. Place one or two (or more) pillows for comfort. Once in a comfortable position, they will open their legs, allowing the other to sit back into them. Place a pillow between the two of you. They can either lie down or lean to one side. From there, the person at the back can wrap their arms around you or not. You can engage in hair play as well.

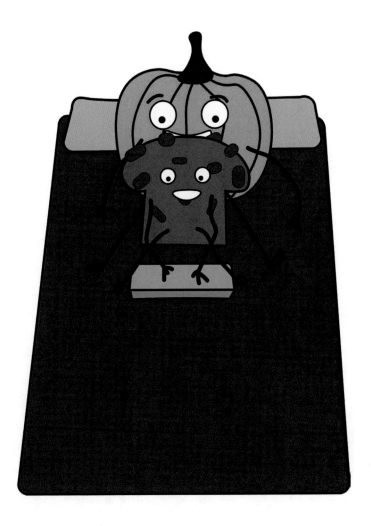

THE BACKBOARD

Stuck living in a studio space with your loved one and have no couch? Or, do you have a project deadline that requires you to work late into the night, but your partner needs to go to sleep? You do not want to interfere with them from going to sleep. That is why this is a priceless 'best of both worlds' situation when living in a small space.

HOW TO:

Have the person rest on their side, either facing towards or away from you. Try to use them as a backrest, headrest, or support for yourself. If using as a headrest, the stomach, chest, thighs or hips can be used. This is useful if wanting to work on an activity while the other wants to sleep or read. Perfect for when both want to do two separate activities. If one is trying to sleep and the other is watching a show - it would be a sneaky position to escape their computer light and find darkness. Just turn away from them while still supporting them.

The Backboard is suitable for partners who have opposite work schedules and need to sleep at different times. It is the best of both worlds!

HEAD PLAY

You were cuddling with *Never Let Me Go* and you began to fall asleep - but you did not want to change positions because you were comfortable in your loved one's arms. This is an excellent next step. Simply move forward until there is enough room to lie back into your loved one's legs or pillow.

HOW TO:

Similar to *Never Let Me Go*, *Head Play* is the version when they decide to rest their head and sleep. Be careful though, this can cause the person who is sitting up, to have their legs fall asleep. If both parties are uncomfortable, try placing a pillow under the head for more comfort.

If the person who is sitting wants to help the person fall asleep, they can play with their head and hair. It will help them fall asleep if they are struggling, and put a smile on their face. It is also a good comforting position if they are feeling down. Continue playing with their hair and squeeze their body gently with your legs.

CONCLUSION

Some of my favourite memories with my loved ones were coming home from a long day of work, exhausted, and resting my feet on the couch or bed. We watched a movie as they played with my hair, calming me down from my day. These special moments have helped me build positive relationships with people that I care about. It's times like these that I will cherish. If someone could make me feel calm, relaxed, and turned my horrible day into something positive – it made me believed that they had a superpower. Knowing how wonderful those special moments made me feel, I wanted to share my experiences with you. Sharing those loving super powers with others is what you can do by using *The Cuddling Sutra*.

I never used to be a cuddler. I even disliked hugs from friends. Over time, they kept persevering and now I cannot stop hugging or cuddling. I hope that this book will have a positive impact on your relationships and for your self care. I think that cuddling is important for a healthy mind, body and soul, and we need to practise it more often.

Did you master all these positions? Fear not! I am working on a more advanced, experimental cuddling book as well.

From the beautiful cuddlers in this book to you, let's *Group Hug!*

Published in 2021
@thecuddlingsutra

Made in the USA
Las Vegas, NV
17 November 2024

12020611R00057